DEDICATION

In Memoriam

Joan Ashton Clark
March 1, 1931 – March 25, 2015
m. December 1, 1986

ENDORSEMENTS

Seed Voices, by Sheldon Clark, invites readers to celebrate some of life's transitional moments. These poetic narratives are raw, authentic, and impactful. As one reads them, the author invites readers into his world. In turn, they encourage readers to reflect on their life-journeys and those memorable incidents that were particularly instructive. *Seed Voices* offers *aides-mémoires* to be present in the moment, to honor experience, and to embrace the varied richness life provides.

Melissa Grimaldi
Health Aging & Society BA, McMaster University (2020)
Graduate Certificate, Fanshawe College (2023)
Compliance Manager, Highgate Retirement Residence
Sofia Grimaldi
Honours BA Health Management, Wilfrid Laurier University (2025)
Receptionist/ Administrative Assistant, Highgate Retirement Residence

Red Smith (1905-1982), American author, famously said that good writing is easy: "You simply sit down at the typewriter, open your veins, and bleed. Writing that moves us is ruthlessly honest and comes from a place of vulnerability; it requires courage as well as wisdom and insight." The poems in *Seed Voices* are that kind of writing. They are the distillation of a lifetime of thought and reflection that embody Wordsworth's ideal: "The spontaneous overflow of powerful feelings: it takes its origin from emotion recollected in tranquility."

Chuck Roth, B. Math, Waterloo University (1977)
M. Sc. Math, McMaster University (1987)
Retired computer programmer, Bunzl Canada, Burlington, Ontario

Sheldon Clark's poems are vivid, telling, and evocative. He invites us to join him on significant occasions where he gives voice. In our listening, we are carried by the meaning he suggests in that particular moment, always in the direction of personal growth and learning. *Seed Voices* deepens our listening to a place where we find ourselves suddenly standing with the author, in a moment in time, shoulder to shoulder, heart to heart, and soul to soul. Bravo!

Rev. Dr. F. Gardiner Perry, D. Min.
Ecumenical Theological Center, Detroit, MI (1990)
Swedenborg School of Religion, Newton, MA (1979)
BA Dartmouth (1971)
Instructor: Practical Theology at the Center for Swedenborgian Studies
at the Graduate Theological Union, Berkeley, CA

In *Seed Voices*, Sheldon Clark invites us into a life through brief anecdotes that are windows into the things that have stuck in his mind and echoed in his heart. The book is written in sections that progress over time. At the outset, we are shown glimpses of life in specific brief moments: childhood memories, memories of becoming a parent, and glimpses of a child becoming. By the end, the poems are more abstract, reflective, and general, addressing broader questions such as service, anger, and non-violence. Each poem paints a picture of a particular experience, within which one finds themes that are universal. This is a particular story, but also an example of self-reflection for all of us.

Christine L. Hitchcock, Ph.D.
Mathematics, BSc (Hons), McMaster University (1986)
Psychology, MA, University of Toronto (1987)
Experimental Psychology, PhD, University of Toronto (1992)

ACKNOWLEDGEMENTS

Seed Voices are memories and mediations. Each offering is derived from admiration for those who quietly serve others, significant educational experiences, and my imagination. Gratitude to Sherita Kay Clark (nee Flack, 1941–2019); Thomas Douglas Clark (1930–2006); Joan Ashton Clark (1931–2015), equestrian, teacher, friend, and spouse (m. author, 1986–2015); Melissa Grimaldi; Sofia Grimaldi; Dr. Quentin Hardy (1919–2011), pediatrician; The Rev. John F. Lockyer; Amber C. McPhail; Rev. Dr. F. Gardiner Perry; and, inspiration from: *A Year With Thomas Merton*, selected and edited by Jonathan Montaldo; *The Return of the Prodigal Son,* by Henri J. M. Nouwen; and, *R. S. Thomas Uncollected Poems,* edited by Tony Brown and Jason Walford Davies.

Sheldon H. Clark
2025

PREVIOUS PUBLICATIONS

Logos for the Journey, 2024
Water Voices (with Amber C. McPhail), 2023
Fire Voices (with Amber C. McPhail), 2022
After the Fire A Still Small Voice (with Catherine Farquhar), 2022
Still Voices (with Ed VandenDool), 2021
Voices Extended (with Neil Paul), 2016 and 2021
Poetry and Prayer Sketches (with George S. Keltika), 2008, 2013, and 2021

Published by: **Rock's Mills Press**
Oakville, Ontario, Canada
www.rocksmillspress.com
For information, including orders, contact us at: customer.service@rocksmillspress.com

© 2025 by Sheldon H. Clark
Imagery by Sheldon H. Clark, Avery P. Gilbert, Amber C. McPhail, Ryan W. McPhail, or sourced from Public Domain. All rights reserved.

PREFACE

The poems and meditations in *Seed Voices* were written in gratitude for encounters I had between the 1950's and the present, in the complex-simplicity of being friend, parent, teacher, pastor, and perpetual student.

Seed Voices are present as life begins and ends. The Sower in the parable sows seeds by the wayside, in marginal land, and in fertile soil. Regeneration is potential. *Seed Voices* was gestated in the darkness. One job everyone can do is sow seeds for justice and love. Seeds of injustice, cruelty, and hatred die on barren ground.

Flora emerged from the moist earth toward the light and blossomed, bore fruit, and produced more seed for Creation to enjoy.

Fauna reproduction achieved success. Fish of the sea, birds of the air, beasts of the field, and humankind were born and evolved to delight the Creator.

In the beginning *Seed Voices* are silent. Darkness and silence define their emergence and survival. Survival happens in darkness, light, and sound.

The paradox of life is that living things must die in the natural cycle of 'seeding' so new growth can take place.

Autobiographical details deliver the authority of experience. Carl Rogers (1902–1987), American psychologist, said, "What is universal is personal, and what is truly personal is also universal." I am mindful that this statement changes the particular to the universal as I wrote, "Memories," "Occasions," and "Time Slips Away" (Tempus Fugit). The personal may jog a memory for someone else, which metaphorically connects the poet's voice and the reader's residual memory. Truth, in the telling and the remembering, is the common denominator that makes the poetic story universal.

Opening and closing prayers are statements of transcendence. School days may recall happiness and sorrow. The statement, "Life's passages are love shared" (CDS-Day 1), is a statement about relational joys and sorrows. Death is a recurring theme particularly apparent in "The Wall," "Derelict," Puffs of Ashes," "Design," and "Air-Earth-Water-Fire."

Sheldon

CONTENTS

Dedication
Endorsements
Acknowledgements
Preface
Contents

MEMORIES

Opening Prayer
Be Still
Come and See
May I Help You?
November 24, 1982, The Fire
CDS – Day 1

OCCASIONS

Love is Hard to Understand
Rambler
The Wall
Anger
The Sower
Derelict

TIME SLIPS AWAY

Non-Violence
Service
Puffs of Ashes
Design
Air-Earth-Water-Fire
Closing Prayer

MEMORIES

OPENING PRAYER

Let the words of my mouth,
And the meditation of my heart,
be acceptable in thy sight, O Lord,
my strength, and my redeemer.
Psalm 19:14

Creator Spirit,
You Have blessed us with first motions
of air, earth, water, and fire.
You bless us in abundance, and give us freedom
to be tender stewards of Your gifts.

We pray for gentle reminders
to cultivate this Garden
as You would have us do
with compassion, forgiveness, and love
to one another.
Amen.

BE STILL

"Be still. Quiet your minds," a beloved teacher's gentle words.
    Cool breeze and bright sun inspired robins, cardinals,
    sparrows, bluebirds, even crows to sing and caw.
    They were neither still nor quiet until ...
    Bird minds focused on song and sustenance.

In the classroom old glass in double-hung windows
    cast prism colors on antique desks,
    across bowed foreheads, rested in sunbeams
    on the floors' century and-a-half old patina.
    The inner active silence deepened.

Out-of-doors songsters quieted, too.
    Hearts and minds focused on inner nourishment
    as the Light filled waiting spirits with a calming
    peace beyond understanding.
    The bell rang, lifted the spell sounding earthly reality.

Students rose, gathered books, and filed into the hallway.
    Their quiet minds heard distant birdsong.
    The mystical spell achieved hallowedness.
    Their quiet quest for Goodness, Truth, and Beauty had
    revealed the Still Small Voice.

COME AND SEE YOUR DAUGHTER

"Please wait in the lounge," Dr. Quentin Hardy spoke quietly.
Mum quickly was wheeled to surgery.
Lamaze study and breathing exercises fled into bright light.
Obediently, I waited quietly, silently.
"Mother and child are doing well."
"Come and see your daughter."
Eyes closed. Wispy hair. Swaddled. She was a bundle of certainty.
Mimsy smiled through her lengthy tiring labor.
Emergency. C section. Delivery. Relief.
"I love you."
"She's healthy, a beautiful baby."
I had to leave.

Rest.
        Rest.
                Rest.

"And, the Rest is History."

MAY I HELP YOU?

Epiphany.

The northside stable aisle was light and shadows.

A silhouetted figure materialized.

Paddock boots clicked on the cement aisle

and strode toward the opposing entrance.

I saw her, ducked under the stable's security board

as though drawn by instinct toward the lady.

We stopped a few feet apart halfway up and down.

"May I help you," she said.

"Yes," I said.

Forever changed,

"'til death do us part."

November 24, 1981 THE FIRE

The Pickering College Fire was not a drill.
Drill experience kicked in immediately.
Before the fire brigade even arrived,
Pickering people were present and accounted for.

Fire trucks went front and back of the smoldering roof.
Quiet calm stilled the smoke-filled air.
Faculty's quick thinking protected files, valuable paintings, library books,
Essentials and incidentals, personal belongings, and common property.
Volunteer local parents and townspeople rallied to care for displaced people.
The common good was uncommonly well-organized.
Safety first. The Dining Hall was the refuge.
Immediate global communications relieved anxious parents.
Safe. Secure. Organize. Arrange. Coordinate. Manage.
Today is now.
Tomorrow is tomorrow and tomorrow and tomorrow.
The Pillars will survive.
The people of Pickering will persevere.
Once settled comfort food was provided.
The drama of flames shooting from the roof,
Filmed for world consumption ended.
The building fire was out.
Hearts on Fire to live adventurously had begun.
Silent reverent stillness embraced several hundred people.
Night fell on all.
The dawn beckoned.

Special people were safe in their new homes in Newmarket and nearby.
Pet animals were safe, cared for by animal-lover friends.
Friends checked in.
Professionally and personally, I knew,
Everyone had a place and everyone was in their place.
Silence like the night descended embracing everything.
"Tomorrow is just a day away."

CDS – DAY 1

I drove our daughter to Country Day School (CDS) for her first day of grade one.
September's sky was clear.
We chattered happily past ponies, horses, and familiar fields.
Arrival.
"I love you, Dad."
"I love you, too. See you at pick-up time."
Out she got out confident to greet new friends.
Her teacher called her to meet other new students.
I drove a short distance north on Dufferin,
stopped by the side of the road to dry tears.
I bore no other title, just "Dad."
Life's passages are love shared.
Tynedale's barn was a comforting destination.
I went there to weather this daughter's rite of passage.
Work beckoned.
Later, I would take our 'confident wonder' to Tynedale to ride Rambler.
"How was day one?"
"I loved it."

OCCASIONS

LOVE IS HARD TO UNDERSTAND

Mulock Side Road, between Yonge St. and Bathurst, was quiet one afternoon. Amber and I were traveling west to her mom's house at Snowball Corners.
"Your mom and I care deeply about you. We love you."
   "I know, Dad."
"Our separation is not your fault."
   "I know, Dad. You two are just different."
"We shall do everything we can to give you a good life."
   "Thanks, Dad."
"What do you want to be when you grow up?"
   "A psychiatrist. I want to understand why people get angry."
I glanced sideways at the little girl.
I thought, "Where did that adult come from?"
Sometimes love is hard to understand.
   We made the lefthand turn onto Bathurst in silence.
Silence is not empty.
   We were surrounded by a protective embrace.
A car sped past going in the opposite direction.
   "What are you going to do this afternoon?"
"Probably hang out with mom, have dinner, do homework, and sleep."
   "Tomorrow, after school, please take me to Tynedale to ride Rambler."
"Okay."

RAMBLER

She is ready. A Beautiful day.

Blue sky, blue shirt, white clouds, a white shirt, white jump standards, white breeches, white saddle pad, white string girth, and white pony socks initiated the portrait's patterns. Her smile, ramrod straight back, heels down in tall black boots, head erect under a black hunt cap, and black leather gloves focused visual patterns.
Position alert. She kept three straight lines from bit through hands to the elbows; shoulders, hips, heels; and hands, knees, toes revealed pony club expertise.
Clean bridle, saddle, and well-groomed pony completed the visual effect.
Then, the eye transfers to the background lead-line lesson in motion. A young child is looking up-and-ahead in learning to balance in the saddle at the walk.
This equestrian portrait combines stillness. Near motionless clouds slipped along. Anticipation waited for quietly "riding off" before visiting the Wizard's Tree, then Spring's white trilliums in the woods, and cantering along the Green Lane.
The portrait is caught by the camera; a moment in time. It captured memories of four early years of riding lessons, independent practices, happy experiences, and the desire to show and win!
A proud 84-year-old father, 42 years later, gazes at the portrait of his 7-year-old "champion."

She is ready. A Beautiful day.

THE WALL

I sense the eternal as
inviting, welcoming, patiently waiting.

My bedroom wall is not a foot away.
It is next to my bed on which
I sleep, eat, breathe, live, and
muse on memories and dreams.

My wall has three true dimensions
Height, width, and length and a
fourth dimension of beautiful memories.

The wall's dimensions hug carpeted
flooring and a white ceiling
that define the entrance/exit.
The wall is pale grey. The trim is white.

The wall bears sunshine, moonlight,
And playful dancing shadows.
The wall opens to schools, life choices,
opportunities to explore the world,
and the desire to be of service to others.

"Do no harm."
I am an idealist enchanted by what could be.

The wall is a protective artifice,
like China's wandering wonder,
Rome's defensive stone piles
from Mediterranean warmth to
England's wet-cold-stone sheep enclosures.

I see Lincoln's Kentucky split rails,
Frost's Vermont 'good fences' being 'good neighbors'
and flagstone paths and raised garden frames;
thoughtful mud-free borders.

I remember the joys of romance,
of love, children, family life,
and simple caring that encouraged
my better angels to prevail.

I remember finding ways to be transformed
with mindfulness and compassion.
I inhale and exhale slowly.
I have become physically weak
but feel ever so strong mentally and spiritually.

I sense the Eternal Presence as
inviting, welcoming, patiently waiting
for all walls to vanish.

ANGER

Anger wraps its wickedness in carapaces of pride.
"Because I say so."
Anger sees opposition as an opportunity.
"Shut up!"
Anger pushes its barbed quills deeper.
"There's nothing to discuss."
Anger turns its screw of spite to scar the psyche.
"It's all your fault!"
Anger's blindness is accusatory.
"You just don't care."
Anger desecrates body and soul.
"Don't act so superior."
Anger's cancer metastasizes everywhere.
"I feel awful all over."
Anger's victim is broadsided.
"I don't know what's wrong?"
Anger attacks, churning well-being, into misery.
"You're the one who's sick."
Anger's pain is physical, gut-wrenching.
"I want to vomit."
Anger provokes fear, tears, despondency.
"I don't know what to do?"

Anger's eyes glaze over, ears deafen, speech is squashed.
"Get real."
Anger's provocation may well up from subconscious inadequacy.
"I feel helpless."
Anger strikes out seeking dominance from impotency.
"I am in control."
Anger's intensity is an out-of-control rag.
"It's you, you, you!"
Anger builds upon itself until gasping for breath.
"You just don't understand me."
Anger breaks its stranglehold.
"Just go away. I feel like dying."
Anger asks: "What was that all about?"
"I don't know?"

THE SOWER

"Listen!"
The cold late January Galilean dawn beckoned.
Jude's head scarf offered necessary warmth.
His calloused fingers readied wheat grain to broadcast measured
portions from his shoulder sling through his funnelled fingers.

"Watch!"
The tiny field had been prepared after the late rains with ox and plough.
On this New Year's Day, Jude cast the seeds in repetitive arcs
as he walked along the furrows. Wind drifts helped disperse the grain,
falling where it may through the humid air.

"Smell!"
The pungent temptation of ploughed earth and scattered seeds
arose from the hard-packed borders, the exposed limestone rocks,
the thorny brushes, and most assuredly from the open field.
A multitude of Tiberian sparrows celebrated instinctively.

"Feel!"
Jude felt the weight of obligation to feed his family,
have enough left over to share, and bask in the joy of effort.
He felt light-hearted performing this invigorating work
knowing in several months the fruit of his labor would be rewarded.

"Taste!"
The rising sun warmed the well-trodden paths.
Jude, imagined freshly baked loaves, as he methodically
crisscrossed the fertile field of being and becoming
in anticipation of a bountiful harvest.

"Shalom"

Based on 'The Sower' (Le Semeur), by James Tossot (1836–1902)
The painting may be viewed at the Brooklyn Museum, NYC

DERELICT

Asleep, drunk, fallen halfway between the curb and the dirty road,
he looked dead under the lamppost. This was not a movie scene.
Dad had parked the car in a vacant lot near the Cleveland Public Auditorium.
We were walking this early wintery 1949 night in anticipation of enjoying
The American and Canadian Sport and Outdoor Show.

Dr. Clark, our mother, checked for pulse and breath.
She confirmed the derelict was alive.
My brother and I could smell the whisky fumes and vomit from several feet away.
This cold evening, we saw a person in need of care.
Dad went into the Bar to telephone for an ambulance.
We waited outside.
Cigar, cigarette smoke, and stale beer exited as he entered.
Tobacco smoke followed him into the cold when he came out.
The man had not moved.
We heard the siren.

Mom and Dad conferred with the medics.
They checked the man and lifted him into the ambulance.
They thanked our parents for their Good Samaritan concern.
Jesus' parable learned in First Day School was practical and timeless.
The juxtaposition of these two starkly different scenes has never been forgotten.
The contemporary need for immediate intervention was automatic.
Compassion was essential to redress the woes of the man on the street.
He sought escape from his reality of poverty through addiction.
Other revelers sought escape from the humdrum by indulging in the fantastic.

Today, at the end of the first quarter of the 21st century, timeless human aspirations have not changed. Loving relationships with hopes and dreams are born afresh against a backdrop of poverty amidst plenty, the pursuit of peace against the angst of perpetual war, and the desire for life, when there is so much evidence of fear and death. We, the people of the world family, want to embrace personal, family, and community transformation merely to survive. Like refugees and immigrants, tradesmen and farmers, scientists and engineers, artists and poets, everyone can show the best of human values, love, compassion, courage, gratitude, kindness, mercy, vision, humility, selflessness, self-control, transcendence, wisdom, and what is meant by heart.

TIME SLIPS AWAY

NON-VIOLENCE

Non-violence is a way of life, not a destination.
    The aim for living a non-violent life is peace.

Non-Violence within is instinctive for physical survival.
    Do I practice Simple Living so Others may Simply Live?

Non-Violence within is instinctive for psychological survival.
    Do I practice Affirmative Self-Care?

Non-Violence within is instinctive for spiritual survival.
    Do I practice disciplined spiritual reflection?

Non-Violence within may be instinctive social survival.
    Do I practice Random Acts of Kindness?

Non-Violence within may be instinctive of defense and of offense.
    Do I practice Reconciliation as a Matter of Love?

Non-Violence within is instinctive as a counter to internal violence.
    Do I practice Contemplative Meditation?

Non-Violence within is instinctive for marrying word and deed.
    Do I practice Faith in Action.

Non-Violence within may be instinctive of calmness.
    Do I practice developing Quietude?

Non-Violence within is instinctive to dispel anger.
    Do I practice Magnanimity?

Non-Violence within is instinctive for the formation of inner peace.
    Do I practice Equanimity?

        Blessed are the peacemakers, for they shall be called the children of God.

SERVICE

Service sees needs.
Service is creatively helpful.
Service examines alternatives.
Service is the predilection to caring.
Service is sympathetic shepherding.
'Wisdom' is the sine qua non of service.

Service is noble.
Service is considerate.
Service is heart-warming.
Service assumes responsibility.
Service is inspirational without limitation.
Inasmuch as ye have done it … ye have done it unto Me.

Service listens to the Spirit.
Service is extraordinary attentiveness.
Service practices predictable consistency.
Service separates the essential from the incidental.
Service incorporates and respects others' initiatives.
Service enlarges our expectations to incorporate theirs.

Service is ubiquitous.
Service occurs anytime anywhere.
Service obeys the calls for diversity.
Service artfully, lovingly, and selflessly benefits.
Service intermingles among individuals and groups.
Serving others serves three, their neighbour, themself, and Me.

PUFFS OF ASHES

The day of the Lord will come as a thief in the night
... and the works that are therein shall be burned up.
II Peter 3:10

A whisper teases conjecture.
Does the tolling bell toll?
The taunting continues.
The bell tolls.
Alone I am not bereft.
Does the final consummation arrive?
"No. No. No. No!"
The bell tolls.
What? What? What?
Does extinction preclude compassion?
"Signifying nothing."
The bell tolls.
Alone I am not afflicted by fear.
Does the Ark alter the Flood?
"The Fire next time."
The bell tolls.
Alone I am asking,
Does innocence revert "through the Looking Glass?"
"Second childhood and mere oblivion."
The bell tolls.
Alone I am with antique Shadows.
What remains?
"For dust you are and to dust you will return."
The bell tolls.
Alone I am not deprived of sensibility.
Do body and soul just evaporate?
"I am the Alpha and the Omega."
The bell tolls.
Alone I am in the manicured rose garden.
Puffs of ashes waft to earth.
A single cloud drifts seaward.
The bell tolls.

DESIGN

Design is captured in sightless leaves
icy spider-webbed windows
springtime's gamboling energy
summertime's endeavours
long days short nights
Fortune's wheel transcends privilege or poverty.

    Design varies by happenstance, circumstance
    ridges, savannahs, jungles, ice floes,
    monsoons, temperate climes, urban clamor
    the unpredictable mystery. Warning!
    "Expect the Unexpected".
    Death prepares for rebirth.

        Design is surgically precise in execution
        spontaneous like jazz variations
        ominous as slow-motion accidents
        fatal as rock climbing slips-and-falls
        evil as blunt force to body, head, or heart
        the Reaper awaits aloof.

            Design endows visions dreams possibilities
            attentive to Love's omnipresence
            embracing gestation's darkness
            birthing hope at dawn's light
            welcoming faith, grace
            sans pareil Spirit's Being.

                Design surrounds Death's fidelity
                partners hold its birthright in trust
                inaudible expression
                decisive separation crossed
                we are here-and-now
                beings loving beings.

There's a special providence in the fall of a sparrow. If it be now, 'tis not to come; if it be not to come, it will be now; if it be not now, yet it will come. The readiness is all.

(Shakespeare, *Hamlet*. V. ii.)

AIR-EARTH-WATER-FIRE

Air
    Deep space silent beyond sensory perceptions teases curiosity.
        Earth's air quality fluctuates between healthy and toxic depending.
            Expanding horizons disappear mysteriously into the void
                reappearing in time-warped possibilities for E.T. life.
                    Smiling imaginings strive to chart conjectures.

Earth
    Grasses, berries, fruit, vegetables, meats quench hunger pangs.
        Sun-drenched rock faces challenge would-be explorers,
            harbor moss, and crawly creatures.
                Vast arctic permafrost tundra appears lifeless.
                    Smiling imaginings authenticate frozen dinosaurs.

Water
    Springs, streams, lakes, reservoirs, rain, slake thirsty souls.
        Moist grey-green mosses disintegrate even granite.
            Springs, brooks, streams may find their way downhill.
                Scarcity, contamination, disenfranchise billions.
                    Smiling imaginings envision freedom from want.

Fire
    Light flashes, St. Elmo's fire, startled land-lubbers and sea-farers alike.
        Destruction precedes new growth in forested amazement.
            Mythologically, Phoenix perpetually arises from its ashes.
                Imaginings smile at survival despite carnages.

CLOSING PRAYER

Creator Spirit,
Your Peace is destroyed.
Your Air is polluted.
Your Earth is raped.
Your Water is contaminated.
Your Fire has become an instrument of death.

Mea Culpa.

Creator Spirit,
In Your Mercy forgive us.
In Your Mercy grant us breath.
In Your mercy grant us compassion.
In Your Mercy lead us to cleansing fire
To feed, to warmth, to see Your Shining Light.

Creator Spirit,
Fallen and undeserving as we are,
We empty ourselves of iniquity,
To be as You intended us to be,
Purveyors of blessedness
To all Creation.
Amen.

"The earth is the Lord's, and the fulness thereof; the world, and they that dwell therein."
Psalm 24:1

www.ingramcontent.com/pod-product-compliance
Lightning Source LLC
Chambersburg PA
CBHW061114070526
44583CB00027B/3292